D0398808

WHICH JESUS?

OTHER BOOKS BY TONY CAMPOLO

Carpe Diem

Following Jesus Without Embarrassing God

It's Friday, but Sunday's Comin'

Let Me Tell You a Story

20 Hot Potatoes Christians Are Afraid to Touch

You Can Make a Difference

WHICH JESUS?

TONY CAMPOLO

W PUBLISHING GROUP™

www.wpublishinggroup.com

A Division of Thomas Nelson, Inc.
www.ThomasNelson.com

Copyright © 2002 Tony Campolo. All rights reserved. No portion of this book may be reproduced, stored in a retrieval system, or transmitted in any form or by any means—electronic, mechanical, photocopy, recording, or any other—except for brief quotations in printed reviews, without the prior permission of the publisher.

Published by W Publishing Group, a division of Thomas Nelson, Inc., P. O. Box 141000, Nashville, Tennessee 37214.

Unless otherwise indicated, Scripture quotations used in this book are from the King James Version.

Scripture quotations marked NKJV are from The New King James Version copyright © 1979, 1980, 1982, Thomas Nelson, Inc., Publishers.

Library of Congress Cataloging-in-Publication Data

Campolo, Anthony.
Which Jesus? / by Tony Campolo.
     p. cm.
  ISBN 0-8499-4403-1
  1. Love—Religious aspects—Christianity. I. Title.
BV4639 .C26 2003
241'.4—dc21   2002154123

Printed in the United States of America

03 04 05 06 07 PHX 9 8 7 6 5 4 3 2 1

*In memory of my nephew Raymond P. Scull,
who so much wanted to follow Jesus Barjoseph
in ministry to the poor and oppressed*

CONTENTS

Acknowledgments   ix

Introduction: Getting into the Story   xi

1. The Two Messiahs   1

2. The Way of Power vs. The Way of Love   10

3. Which Jesus Do You Want?   29

4. Love Can Do Amazing Things   44

5. Love's Supremacy over Power   60

6. How to Experience the Miracle of Love   69

Epilogue: Are You Ready to Do Love?   77

ACKNOWLEDGMENTS

A special thanks to Valerie Hoffman, who typed the manuscript for this book. Also a round of applause to Jennifer Stair for the fine editing job that made it ready for publication. Much gratitude to Laura Kendall, of W Publishing Group, who orchestrated getting this book into print. Most of all, thanks to my wife, Peggy, who spent endless hours improving my writing and helping me find the best way to say what I wanted to say.

GETTING
INTO THE STORY

This is the story of two men named Jesus, each of whom claimed to be the Messiah. They were contemporaries, and their lives were so interwoven that it has been said that the destiny of each was wrapped up in the destiny of the other.

The Jesus who was born of the Virgin Mary, who suffered under Pontius Pilate, and who was crucified, risen, and is alive today, is the true Messiah. He is the one ordained to be the Savior of the world. He is the Jesus who came to save the world through sacrificial love.

The other Jesus of our story—Jesus Barabbas—also claimed to be a messiah, but his way of saving the people of Judah was by means of armed revolution. The kingdom Jesus Barabbas sought to establish was not to be created by love, but rather through the exercise of militaristic power. This Jesus offered the ancient Jews a vision of deliverance that promised freedom from the Roman authorities who dominated them. But his way of achieving that end would be through the sword.

I first heard about the possibility that Barabbas might have had Jesus as a first name during my seminary days. My professor of New Testament said that he thought it strange that when Pilate asked the crowd to choose which man they wanted to be set free during the Jews' annual Passover celebration, he did not use Barabbas's first name, which would have been the expected thing to do. Since Barabbas means "son of Abbas," it would have been confusing to refer to him only by his surname, especially if his father had more than one son. Might it be, suggested my professor, that Barabbas's first name was also Jesus, and Pilate was trying to differentiate between two men who bore the same first name?

I began to consider how ironic it would be if my professor were right. Over the years, I have tried to track down concrete evidence that Barabbas's first name really was Jesus. I have come upon a number of hints and suggestions, but I have not yet found the convincing evidence that historians require. I can't prove that the given name of the man we call Barabbas was Jesus, but I have come to believe that it was. And that belief has given rise to this little book.

By the way, the name Barabbas translates as "son of God." That fact, in and of itself, doubles the irony of this story.

Let us look at the differences between these two messiahs as their stories unfold. I have woven their stories together using biblical facts, historical records, and yes, some imagination. But through it all, one question emerges: Which Jesus will you choose to be your Savior and to call the Lord of your life?

ONE

THE TWO MESSIAHS

God's Son, Jesus, had a last name while growing up in Nazareth, insofar as people had last names back then. He went by the name of His surrogate father, Joseph. In Hebrew, His last name was Barjoseph, which means "son of Joseph." But our Savior wasn't the only child in ancient Israel to be given the name Jesus. It was a common name in those days. Jesus is another form of the name Joshua, which means "deliverer" or "savior."

There was another boy named Jesus who was born to a father named Abbas, and so he was called Jesus Barabbas. He, too, lived in the small town of Nazareth, a hotbed for radicals. Young men growing up there were taught to hate the Roman conquerors who dominated their land and defiled all that was sacred in Israel. Like other young boys in Nazareth, Jesus Barabbas loved to hear the stories of Judas Maccabaeus, who defied Israel's oppressors and led a revolution that freed the Jews from tyranny. He dreamed of one day leading another revolution to free Israel from its oppressors.

With role models like Judas Maccabaeus, it is no wonder that Nazareth had the reputation of breeding terrorists. People in Jerusalem, where the Roman conquerors had achieved some degree of accommodation, would often say, "Can any good come out of Nazareth?"

TERRORISTS—THEN AND NOW

Today similarities could be noted between Jesus Barabbas and Osama bin Laden. Each, in his own time, challenged the one superpower that dominated his world, a government that he viewed as oppressing his people. And each man was deemed a hero by that radical element in society whose answer to oppression is violence.

Like Osama bin Laden and his al-Qaeda terrorists, Jesus Barabbas and his followers, known as Zealots, lived in mountain caves. The Zealots would sneak into town, mingle undetected with the mobs of people in the marketplace, use long knives to do their murderous work, and then disappear back into the surrounding mountains. Their targets were Jews who cooperated with the Roman authorities, gained wealth and power by collecting taxes on behalf of their overlords, and compromised their religious traditions in complying with Roman expectations.

In retaliation for the Zealots' acts of terrorism, the Roman captains would send troops into those mountainous regions where these murderers hid to try to flush them out. But the hills and mountains were friends to the terrorists. They knew the terrain, and they knew how to use the caves as vantage points from which to attack and kill any who would dare to follow them there.

Two thousand years later, terrorists in Afghanistan would use similar tactics. Like the followers of Jesus Barabbas, some contemporary religious fanatics delude themselves into thinking that they are the fists of God, banging out justice against a foreign power that they blame for all that is wrong in their land. Both in ancient Israel and in Afghanistan, those killed in the struggle against the powerful, evil foreigners were revered as martyrs.

THE TWO MESSIAHS AT SCHOOL

Let us go back to the childhood of Jesus Barabbas as he grew up in that little town north of Jerusalem called Nazareth. There must have been a certain charisma about him that attracted other boys to his side. As they played their school games, Jesus Barabbas may have pretended to be the leader of a band of would-be commandos who carried out his hit-and-run raids against the occupying enemy army. I can imagine that every day at recess Jesus Barabbas and his boyhood followers acted out make-believe victories over Roman legions, after which they declared themselves to be the heroes of Israel.

But the other Jesus of our story also attended that little one-room schoolhouse in Nazareth. He was not particularly handsome, and He did not carry himself with the arrogant gait of other boys His age. He wasn't rough or loud, and at times He seemed a bit distant, as though He were in another world. This other Jesus never played in the war games that were led by Jesus Barabbas. To the rest of the boys at school, He may have seemed a bit too serious.

The other boys did not like that He never joined them when they had their fun tormenting younger and weaker children. In reality, Jesus Barjoseph seemed to have a special affection for the losers and nerds of His school. When He was around, the other boys tended not to bother their usual prey—not because Jesus Barjoseph threatened them, but because He could look into their eyes in a piercing way that brought out the best in them. In spite of His being different, the other boys found something intriguing and attractive in Jesus Barjoseph. In His own way He, too, had charisma.

Undoubtedly the rabbi, who was their teacher, occasionally got the two boys named Jesus mixed up when he called the roll at the beginning of the school day. But Jesus Barabbas and Jesus Barjoseph were so different that he seldom confused them other than in the calling of the roll. Both of the boys named Jesus were excellent students, and each had a special interest in the ancient kings of Israel—especially King David—but in such different ways! Jesus Barabbas wanted to be the David who was the conquering warrior, whereas Jesus Barjoseph noted the deep spirituality of David and even memorized the psalms of that poet king. The rabbi knew that each of these favored boys would grow up to be special.

It was obvious that Jesus Barjoseph was destined to be much more than a carpenter. The rabbi was sure that this Jesus would one day be a teacher of the Law and the Prophets. This unusual boy had a fascination with Scripture, and the rabbi was sure that he had never had a student who spent more time studying God's Word.

As they grew up, the boys developed an affection for each

other. Jesus Barabbas always made sure that the roughnecks in the school never picked on his friend—not that Jesus Barjoseph couldn't take care of Himself, but because Jesus Barabbas had noticed that this other Jesus, if struck, would just turn the other cheek and allow His tormentor to hit Him again. Each of the boys noticed the uniqueness of the other, and, different as they were, they seemed to have a mutual respect.

My Father's Business

When the boys were twelve years old, the family of Jesus Barabbas and the family of Jesus Barjoseph joined the other townspeople from Nazareth to travel to Jerusalem, the holy city of the Jews. There the boys would go through what we call today the bar mitzvah. Each would stand before the congregation in the temple and declare, "Today I am a man!"

The trips to and from Jerusalem for such celebrations were always fun times for the children. The boys and girls would run ahead of their parents and the town elders. They would laugh and play. Like all youngsters everywhere, the boys would flirt with the girls by taunting them, while their parents halfheartedly would call for them to stop.

The walks to and from Jerusalem also were good times for the adults, opportunities for storytelling and remembering. On one occasion, so caught up were they in this happy time of visiting on the way home that, at first, they did not notice the absence of Jesus Barjoseph. It wasn't until the end of the day, when the community stopped their journey and settled down to sleep through the night, that Mary and Joseph realized their son was not with them. They had supposed their Jesus was with the other young men. They were shocked to discover that He wasn't with Jesus Barabbas. The boys were so different, but they liked each other and usually hung out together.

In a panic, Mary and Joseph hustled back to Jerusalem, fearing the worst but hoping for the best. When they got to Jerusalem, they sought everywhere for their son, but only when they looked in the least likely place did they find Him. Jesus Barjoseph was in the courtyard of the temple in deep conversation with the scholars of the Torah, who regularly gathered there to discuss the teachings of Moses and the prophets. For a moment the parents stood in wonder because their Jesus had these learned men enthralled. His questions were so profound that the scholars were amazed.

Then Joseph interrupted, pulled Jesus away, and said,

"Where have you been? You had your mother and me worried sick." Jesus Barjoseph answered in a way that must have stunned His parents: "Did you not know that I must be about My Father's business?"

What does He mean by that? Why is my dear son so strange? Why isn't He like the other boys, like Jesus Barabbas? Mary pondered these things in her heart.

A TIME FOR ACTION

The day came when the other Jesus knew that his time for action had come. There had been much talk about restoring the throne of David to its one-time greatness, but Jesus Barabbas knew that talk alone would accomplish nothing. So one evening, he challenged the young men of the town: "Let's be bold and fight against the Gentile dogs who desecrate the temple in Jerusalem and who unfairly tax us. We'll start the battle, people will rise up and join us, and then together we will march to victory!"

The blood of the others ran hot as Jesus Barabbas spoke, but as Jesus Barjoseph listened to His friend, He grew pensive. He simply added quietly, "Those who live by the sword will die by the sword. The way to overcome their evil is to do good to our enemies and to love them." His words sounded crazy to Jesus Barabbas, as well as to most of the young men of Nazareth.

But time would tell which Jesus was truly a man of action, a man whose deliberate choices would leave a lasting impact on His world and on future generations for the rest of human history.

TWO

THE WAY OF POWER
VS. THE WAY OF LOVE

As the years went by, the two young men named Jesus lost track of each other. Jesus Barabbas, and those who believed in him, seemed to disappear. At first, even his family did not know where he was. But then rumors started coming back to Nazareth, and, in the years that followed, the exploits of Jesus Barabbas and his followers were on the lips of just about everyone in town.

The fame of Jesus Barabbas spread everywhere throughout the surrounding countryside and up through the far reaches of the Golan Heights. This young guerilla fighter and his followers, known as Zealots, became notorious for their hit-and-run attacks on the Roman legions that were supposed to keep the Jews in line. They struck fear in the heart of any person who dared to have dealings with the

Romans—especially the tax collectors, who were despised collaborators with the occupying army. Tax collectors were so threatened by the followers of Jesus Barabbas that they were afraid to venture out at night. Even during the daylight hours they felt unsafe. Who could be sure that in a crowded marketplace one would not bump up against a Zealot ready to mete out capital punishment to those who did business with "the dogs from Rome"?

Jesus Barjoseph also picked up a reputation, but His was very different from that of the radical who had been His childhood friend. Jesus Barjoseph gained His fame as a faith healer and a preacher. As He traveled by foot around the Sea of Galilee, hordes of people chased after Him seeking help. It was said that simply touching the hem of His robe would have a healing effect on even the most seriously ill. If there was fear of Jesus Barabbas on the one hand, there was, on the other hand, a sense of awe when people encountered the other Jesus from Nazareth. It was said of Jesus Barjoseph that He could make the blind to see and the lame to walk. Rumors abounded that someday He would even raise the dead.

There also was a great hubbub about the things that Jesus Barjoseph taught. He talked about the kingdom of God, stating that it was at hand. He spoke of a new social order in which those who were hungry would be fed. He claimed that the oppressed, who wept over the injustices they had to endure at the hands of the rich and the powerful, would soon be delivered and lifted up to the status of royalty. There was even growing talk that this other Jesus of Nazareth might be the long-awaited Messiah of the Jews. While not everyone went that far in their speculations, there was a widespread belief among the Jews that at least He might be the reincarnated son of Elijah the prophet, resurrected from the grave to call people to repentance and to announce that the Messiah would soon be coming.

SAME CONCERNS, DIFFERENT APPROACHES

It is likely that Jesus Barjoseph was somewhat sympathetic to the agenda of Jesus Barabbas. He, too, would have been upset by the way in which the Sadducees compromised with the governing Romans, who were indifferent to so much that the Jews deemed sacred. The two young men must have shared contempt for the sneaky ways in which Herod, whom Jesus Barjoseph once called a "fox" (Luke 13:32), kept his power by playing political games with the Roman oppressors.

They undoubtedly despised the practices of the high priests, who were all too willing to allow the outer court of the temple—a place for Gentiles and women to worship—to be used for merchandising purposes. The haggling and cheating that went on there as people bought and sold the doves and sheep needed for temple sacrifices were scandalous. Thus the two men named Jesus shared a zeal for purifying the temple so that it would once again be totally sanctified, as in the days of King Solomon, to fulfill divine intentions.

Jesus Barjoseph also shared with Jesus Barabbas a certain displeasure with the tax collectors, who not only had become agents for a foreign power, but were often corrupt—forcing the people to pay more than Roman law required and keeping the surplus for themselves. But Jesus Barjoseph always seemed to be appealing to them to change, whereas Jesus Barabbas wanted to kill them.

In spite of their differences, the two young men from Nazareth shared far more than a first name. They had a common zeal for revolutionizing the nation. It was their methods that made them so different. We know that Jesus Barjoseph was not adverse to recruiting the same kind of radicals to be His disciples as were drawn to Jesus Barabbas. On the list of

His chosen twelve apostles was Simon the Zealot (Luke 6:15). It is likely that Peter was a Zealot, too, because when the Roman soldiers came to take Jesus Barjoseph prisoner in the Garden of Gethsemane, Peter, like any true Zealot, quickly drew his knife and cut off the ear of one of them.

The sons of Zebedee, James and John, also were possible Zealots. When they asked to sit on the right and left hand of His throne when Jesus Barjoseph established His kingdom, they showed that they believed in the Zealots' dream of a new political order. There is even reason to suspect that Judas Iscariot was a Zealot, which might help us to understand why he betrayed Jesus Barjoseph. His notorious betrayal may have resulted from his growing disappointment and disillusionment at the failure of Jesus Barjoseph to lead a violent revolution.

THE TEMPTATION OF POWER

To some extent, Jesus Barjoseph found the Zealots' use of power very tempting. It was the temptation to use power rather than sacrificial love to establish His kingdom that Satan saw as his best means to seduce Jesus Barjoseph from His Father's prescribed way of saving the world. Satan told

Him that He would have a following if He would just use His power and turn stones into bread. The evil one then tried to get Jesus Barjoseph to show off His power with a few signs and wonders, such as jumping off the highest pinnacle of the temple and floating gently to the ground. And finally, Satan tempted Him by telling Him He could set up His kingdom simply by using power to impose His will on the world.

Jesus Barjoseph responded in each instance by quoting Scripture and, ultimately, by declaring that He would save the world, not through the exercise of power, but through sacrificial love. He would save the world through the cross. Instead of using coercive power, He would draw people to Himself through His self-giving love on Calvary.

The temptation to use power, rather than love, to carry out His mission was most difficult for Jesus Barjoseph to resist; and when He did overcome it, Satan warned Him that He would have to face this temptation again and again during the course of His ministry. It is this temptation that Jesus Barjoseph had to fight off at Caesarea Philippi when Peter railed against the prophecy that Jesus would have to suffer and die to establish His kingdom. In Peter's call to avoid the cross, Jesus saw the temptation to choose the way of power, so He shouted back at Peter, "Get thee behind me, Satan" (Matt. 16:23). He accused Peter of not understanding God's way of establishing the kingdom and being like the Zealots who thought that the kingdom would be brought in through militaristic power.

At Calvary, Jesus Barjoseph could have yielded to the temptation to come down from the cross and show His power to those who taunted Him. He could have called on ten thousand angels to fight for Him, but He didn't (Matt. 26:53). His disciples may even have mistaken Him for a Zealot when He told them to buy themselves swords, but what He was really doing was warning them that in their preaching of the good news of the kingdom of God, they would have to defend themselves against violent people (Luke 22:38).

All during His days of ministry, Jesus Barjoseph struggled with the temptation to use the power of the sword to deal with the oppressors of the poor and the custodians of an unjust political order. But He steadfastly resisted that temptation, right up to the very end. His commitment to love His enemies and teach His disciples to do the same left no room for violence as a means of dealing with society's evils. He believed that He could overcome evil with good.

To Jesus Barjoseph, the way of the sword would lead the Jews to violent death (Matt. 26:52). That, of course, is what eventually happened to the Zealots. In A.D. 70, they rallied the Jews into a revolution aimed at overthrowing Roman rule, and it was a total disaster. It led not only to the destruction of the temple, but to a rebellion that caused the bloodshed of thousands. Those Zealots might have called themselves "shepherds" who would herd the people to freedom; Jesus Barjoseph knew them to be hirelings who would eventually leave the people to be eaten up by the Roman "wolves" (John 10:12). But while He saw the Zealots' use of violence as dangerous (Matt. 11:12), Jesus Barjoseph must have had some sense of appreciation for their commitment to stand by their cause, even unto death. He may even have wished that His own disciples had their kind of courage.

But Jesus Barjoseph stood firmly on the side of nonviolence. He spent much time explaining that He had no aspirations to use power to overthrow the existing sociopolitical system. Nevertheless, one should not get the idea that Jesus Barjoseph was liked by everyone. Quite to the contrary, He had His share of enemies. Most of the scribes and the Pharisees, along with the priests in the temple, were antagonized by His teachings. It didn't help that He put down their pretentious claims to spiritual superiority and at times ignored the host of rules and regulations that they had dreamed up as they promoted their own particular version of piety and righteousness. Jesus Barjoseph scorned their thousands of prescriptions for piety and dared to reduce all of their laws and regulations to just two lines: "Love the Lord your God with all your heart, with all your soul, and with all your mind" and "Love your neighbor as yourself" (Matt. 22:37, 39). He seemed to cut right through their put-on holiness and expose them as imposters who looked good in outward appearance but whose hearts and minds were filled with deceitful cunning. He said they were like graves in a cemetery, which are covered with flowers and marble tombstones but full of decay beneath the surface (Matt. 23:27).

Whatever Jesus Barjoseph lacked in the way of widespread support from the religious elite was more than compensated for by the massive support He received from those who were poor and socially marginalized. The poor heard Him gladly, and the ostracized—tax collectors, lepers, harlots, and other ceremonially unclean members of society—loved what He had to say. He ignored the religiously dictated condemnation of these outcasts and called them "friends" (Matt. 11:19; John 15:15).

THE TWO ARRESTS

The two men called Jesus were both arrested the same week. Jesus Barabbas was caught during a midnight sweep of the hills just north of Caesarea Philippi. Some poor village people could not resist the promised reward money and told the Roman authorities where he could be found. But the arrest of Jesus Barjoseph was an even greater betrayal, because He was turned in by one of His own inner circle of disciples. Judas Iscariot, whose name would become synonymous with the word *traitor,* had gone to the priests in the temple and told them when Jesus Barjoseph would be in a secluded place where He could be arrested without incident.

Up until the very end, Judas believed that by arranging for Jesus Barjoseph's arrest he could force Him to play His hand and reveal Himself as a militaristic ruler who would destroy Israel's enemies. It was too late when Judas realized that this Jesus would not fight with the sword to bring in His kingdom and that he, Judas, had betrayed a friend who loved him. His miscalculations drove him to suicide.

Justice was quick in those days, and within hours after their respective arrests, both men named Jesus had been found guilty and sentenced to die. The evidence against

Jesus Barabbas was clear and abundant. The verdict was cut-and-dried—death by crucifixion. The case against Jesus Barjoseph, on the other hand, was much more difficult to make, and it was full of ambiguities and contradictions. His accusers, the chief priests of the temple, claimed that He had broken their religious laws and taught others to do the same. But as the case unfolded, it was obvious that Jesus Barjoseph was guilty of breaking none of the laws laid down in the Hebrew Scriptures, but only some of the petty and dubious regulations that the scribes and the Pharisees had added on to them. And even if He had broken some of the religious regulations of these picayune legalists, such crimes were not deemed deserving of crucifixion.

The Roman authorities had a decent judicial system, and there was no way that Jesus Barjoseph deserved the death penalty, even if judged guilty of breaking the religious code of the Jews. But His religious enemies had something going for them when it came to doing Him in. They knew that the Roman authorities had wrongly identified Jesus Barjoseph as a Zealot and that the Romans viewed such militants much as we view Osama bin Laden and his al-Qaeda operatives. Such a terrorist could not be allowed to escape punishment for his seditious activities.

Many of us make much out of the trial of Jesus Barjoseph before the Sanhedrin, but, in reality, that so-called trial was nothing more than a hearing before religious figureheads. Pilate, the potentate for Roman authority, was more than willing to allow the priests of the temple to have their little go-around with Jesus. The hearing would accommodate the religious establishment, and Pilate would still retain judicial authority for himself.

Regardless of beliefs to the contrary, it was the Romans who put Jesus Barjoseph to death. Crucifixion was a Roman device. If the Jews had put Jesus to death, it would have been through stoning, which was the Jews' form of capital punishment. Pilate judged Jesus for the capital crime of being a Zealot leader who, like all the other Zealot leaders of that day, had deemed Himself to be the King of the Jews. Pilate asked Jesus if He were the King of the Jews, intending to usurp Roman rule. Jesus answered in a very evasive way, with a question: "Are you speaking for yourself about this, or did others tell you this concerning Me?" (John 18:34). To Pilate, that response must have seemed more than a bit daring, coming from somebody who was on trial for His life.

Pilate treated Jesus Barjoseph as a Zealot in every respect. He had Him imprisoned as a Zealot and gave Him that status when he presented Him to the people alongside another man who was designated a Zealot—Jesus Barabbas. The Roman ruler was more than a little ambivalent about the whole affair. On the one hand, his own wife had pleaded with him to have nothing to do with condemning Jesus Barjoseph. She'd had a nightmare the night before the trial that had convinced her that condemning this innocent man would be disastrous. On the other hand, the religious leaders were pressuring Pilate to get rid of Jesus Barjoseph. Having realized they could never get Pilate to condemn Jesus Barjoseph to death on such charges as violating the Sabbath or committing blasphemy, they changed their accusations.

First they yelled, "He stirs up the people. Agitators have to be stopped if there's going to be law and order in the land." Then they made the most serious charge of all. "He claims to be a king," they shouted, "as all Zealot leaders do. Therefore this man is an enemy of Caesar." That final charge had to be taken seriously by Pilate, despite the fact that Jesus Barjoseph had claimed that His kingdom was "not of this world" (John 18:36). When Pilate was told that freeing this man would make him no friend of Caesar's, Pilate knew that his decision could have serious consequences for his political future. It was then that he came up with what he considered to be a brilliant solution to his dilemma.

PILATE'S PLAN

During their rule over Israel, the Romans adopted a goodwill gesture that during the Jewish feast of the Passover, a feast in which the Jews celebrated their freedom from Egyptian captivity, a prisoner who had been sentenced to die would be set free. Pilate saw this as an escape from his quagmire. He would shove the responsibility of decision making off on the mob that the religious elite had gathered outside the public balcony of his palace. He would stand before them Jesus Barjoseph and another prisoner who had been accused of being a terrorist. He would ask the people which one *they* wished to have set free. Then the religious leaders of Jerusalem could not go to Rome with word that Pilate had refused to condemn an enemy of Caesar. Nor, on the other hand, could his wife be upset with him for condemning a man whom she felt was innocent.

It was Pilate's prerogative to select the prisoner to stand opposite Jesus Barjoseph when the choice was to be made. As he went over the list of those available for this dubious honor, one name stood out—*Jesus Barabbas!* Surely, thought Pilate, given the choice between these two men, each carrying the name Jesus, the crowd would not choose the threatening terrorist. As much as the Jews wanted their freedom from Rome, Pilate was convinced that they would not choose to set free a murderer who had struck fear in the heart of every decent citizen in Jerusalem.

Pilate must have thought his decision was a stroke of genius. He would give the people a choice between two men, each of whom bore the name that meant "deliverer" or "savior." The one Jesus had sought to create their brave new world by violent revolution. The other had talked about creating the kingdom of God by changing people's hearts and minds. It would be a choice between one man who wanted to create God's kingdom on earth through power and another who wanted to create it through love.

Pilate's sympathies were, of necessity, with Jesus Barjoseph. Why would any ruler want to free someone like Jesus Barabbas, who threatened to destabilize the government? On the other hand, to free Jesus Barjoseph would be to anger the religious establishment, which every politician knows can be fatal to one's career. So he did what politicians down through the ages have done—he polled his constituency. *I'll let the people decide,* he said to himself. *That way, regardless of the decision, it will be in their hands, and not in mine.*

For all the logic that may have gone into Pilate's plan, it had one very basic flaw: Pilate did not understand human nature. He thought that people acted out of logic. However, human beings are more often controlled by irrational emotions, the most important of which is "the will to power." And that misunderstanding set him up for the biggest mistake in history!

Pilate stood on the balcony high above the thousands of citizens of Jerusalem as they raised their fists in the air and prepared to shout their response. On his right was Jesus Barjoseph, and on his left stood Jesus Barabbas.

What must it have been like for those two men to meet after years of separation? What must those two old friends have felt as their eyes met after so much had changed for each of them? Jesus Barabbas undoubtedly was awed by the calm and sense of peace that Jesus Barjoseph radiated in the midst of that turbulent scene. Everyone else was distraught and frantic at that moment, except for Him. Pilate was beside himself with confusion and anxiety. The crowd was fired up to a fevered pitch. The priests of the temple, along with the Pharisees and the Sadducees, were frenzied as they stirred up the crowds to shout against Jesus Barjoseph. Jesus Barabbas may have been the only one who noticed that his childhood friend was the one person who seemed to be in control of His emotions on that horrendous morning.

The moment of decision was at hand. Pilate called out to the people and asked them which Jesus they wanted released and which one they wanted crucified. The choice seemed to be a clear one. The decision ultimately boiled down to a choice between the way of love and the way of power. The convicted men represented not only two very different ways of life, but two completely different solutions to the world's problems and two totally different means for seeking and finding personal security.

Pilate cried out, "Which Jesus do you want? Do you want Jesus Barjoseph, or do you want Jesus Barabbas?"

Without hesitation the crowd yelled back, as though with one voice, "Give us Barabbas!"

"And what shall I do with this other Jesus?" cried Pilate.

"Crucify Him! Crucify Him!" they screamed back.

Pilate must have been stunned by the response. How had this man who, less than a week earlier, had been welcomed by the people of Jerusalem as their Messiah and hailed as King of the Jews come to be so hated? It must have seemed to Pilate as if there were a demonic force behind the crowd, orchestrating their rhythmic chanting and the ugly contortions of their faces. He may have muttered to himself, "Something evil this way cometh."

KING OF THE JEWS

Jesus Barabbas did not know how to react. On the one hand, he must have let out an incredible sigh of relief. He had come so close to the intensely painful death of crucifixion, only to be suddenly spared. Yet there must have been great ambivalence for him, too, because he knew that an innocent man was to die in his place. Jesus Barjoseph was no Zealot. He was no political agitator, and Jesus Barabbas knew it. This was his boyhood playmate who had refused to be part of his schemes to overthrow Roman authority violently and to reestablish King David's throne in Jerusalem. This was the man he had tried to entice into his movement, yet never could. He, a guilty man, would go free, and his innocent childhood friend would die because of his sins. Tradition has it that for the rest of his life Jesus Barabbas would go about begging people for forgiveness, as though this was something *they* could grant him. He did not know that the One who had died in his place had already forgiven him.

Pilate then asked for a basin of water and, with a gesture

aimed at showing his contempt for the rule of the mob, washed his hands and claimed that he had nothing to do with the verdict. Little did he know that history would always deem him guilty of putting to death an innocent man.

Pilate would do one last thing to justify himself as he sentenced Jesus Barjoseph to death. The Romans always put a plaque at the top of the cross when they crucified a man, indicating the crime that the guilty man had committed. Pilate instructed the soldiers to put on that plaque the words, "King of the Jews." However, the priests of the temple wanted to make sure that people saw the statement as nothing more than the arrogant claim of a deluded man, whom they had earlier contended was a bit crazy. So they suggested that Pilate change the sign to read, "He *calls* himself the King of the Jews." But Pilate held fast and said, "What I have written, I have written."

Did Pilate sense that there was more to this Jesus Barjoseph than met his judicial eye? Did he recognize a majesty about this Jesus that evaded his understanding? Perhaps there was an inner voice telling him that this man was more than a man, more than a Zealot pretender to the throne of David, more than the priests and the other religious leaders of the Jews had made Him out to be.

THREE

WHICH JESUS
DO YOU WANT?

Two thousand years have passed since Pilate posed the question to the people in his day: "Which Jesus do you want?" But the question is as crucial today as it was then. Each of us, day by day and hour by hour, is faced with the same dilemma that Pilate created for those who massed beneath his balcony on the painfully decisive day when he asked if they wanted Jesus Barjoseph or Jesus Barabbas. Today every Christian is confronted with the same option: Do we want Jesus Barjoseph, who comes in love, or Jesus Barabbas, who comes in power?

The two men named Jesus were dramatically different from each other. Jesus Barjoseph set aside power in order to save the world through sacrificial love (Phil. 2:5–11). He had the power of God at His disposal, but He gave up that power and took on the limitations of an ordinary human being (v. 7). In the frailty and weakness of His humanity, Jesus Barjoseph was victimized by those who wielded power. The religious and political leaders of the day joined forces against Him and had Him put to death. As a powerless lamb is led to slaughter, He opened not His mouth. He went to the cross without saying a word.

Jesus Barjoseph came into the world in order to change it into a place marked by justice. His mission was to rescue the world from its warring chaos and despair and transform it into a place where His will would be done on earth as it is in heaven. But Jesus Barjoseph would not use coercion or play power games. The citizens of His kingdom would have to *choose* to make Him Lord of their lives in response to His love. No one would be forced to be a part of His kingdom.

The other Jesus was different. His was the way of power. Jesus Barabbas assumed that the only way to deal with enemies was to destroy them. Peace, Jesus Barabbas believed, was brought about by flexing one's muscles and threatening one's adversaries. His version of the golden rule was to do unto others what they might do to you—only to do it first!

The contrast between the way of power adopted by Jesus Barabbas and the way of love as lived out by Jesus Barjoseph is seen in every level of human existence. In family relationships, in life in the church, in the realm of national politics, and especially in the defining of international affairs—the options present themselves. Sadly, the option most often chosen is the way of power. The crowd still cries out for Jesus Barabbas. It can be argued that this has been human nature since the Fall. People understand power, whereas few grasp what love is all about. They feel secure with power, whereas love gives them a sense of vulnerability.

Why is it that the enemies of Jesus Barjoseph often understand what He was about better than do a whole lot of Christians? Certainly Friedrich Nietzsche, the nineteenth-century philosopher who coined the phrase "God is dead," understood the consequences of what Jesus Barjoseph required as a way of life. Nietzsche scorned Jesus' message of love, along with the vulnerability that went with it. Instead, he called upon the youth of Germany to live out their natural impulse of "the will to power." Life is a struggle for survival, contended Nietzsche, and everyone should seek the power that will guarantee him or her victory in that struggle. To Nietzsche, those who let the sentiments of love get in their way become losers. His psychological grasp of who we are led him to believe that everyone has a craving for the power to control things. He saw how threatened we are when we cannot impose our will on the way things are. He believed that most of us feel comfortable about our chances for survival only when we think that we are able to control our own destinies. Love, argued Nietzsche, diminishes our capacity to assert our power, and therefore it should be rejected.

LOVE AND POWER IN THE FAMILY

Sociologists have long been aware that there is an inverse arrangement between power and love. Whoever is exercising the most power in a relationship will be exercising the least love. The reverse is also true: Whoever is expressing the most love in a relationship will be exercising the least power. This is clearly evident as we analyze marriages. If a wife desperately and intensely loves her husband but he does not love her, then he has the most power. Out of love, she will do just about anything he asks of her, but because he does not care whether she leaves or stays, he feels no compulsion to yield to any of her desires. In short, his lack of love has put him in a position to dictate the terms of the relationship.

Husbands very often are afraid to express their love for their wives because, on a subconscious level, they know that doing so would make them vulnerable and cause them to lose some of their power. That is one reason why saying, "I love you," is difficult for many men.

Often when I lead a family life seminar at a church and there is a question-and-answer time, some macho man stands and says, "Doctor, you haven't answered the *real* question— who's supposed to be head of the house?"

I have an urge (which I have never acted out) to answer, "If you were a mature Christian, you wouldn't ask a question like that! The mature Christian never asks who is going to be the master, but always asks who is going to be the servant." That question is the same offensive question that James and John asked Jesus Barjoseph when they inquired, "Master, when You come into Your kingdom, who will sit on Your left hand and who will sit on Your right?" In other words, who will have the *power*? Jesus Barjoseph told them that in His kingdom those who would be masters become servants, and those who aspire to be first must be willing to be last. Being part of His kingdom requires the abandonment of power games.

The ideal marriage is one in which power plays are set

aside and each submits to the other in love (Eph. 5:21). Imagine, if you can, a marriage in which the wife says to her husband, "My dreams and aspirations are only secondary. I want to live my life so that you can actualize *your* dreams and become everything that God expects you to be." To which he responds, "Oh, no! I want to sacrifice myself so that you become all that you can be by the grace of God."

And she comes back with, "Oh, no! I am going to sacrifice myself for you!"—and they have their first fight. That is the only kind of fight the Bible ever tells us to have, because the Bible instructs us to outdo one another in love, with each treating the other better than himself or herself (Phil. 2:3).

When it comes to expressing love, Jesus Barjoseph established the model (Phil. 2:5). He had all the power of God at His disposal, but some two thousand years ago, He surrendered His power in order to express His love for us. The great Creator of the universe, whose power is even now manifested throughout the cosmos, took on human flesh and, in the weakness of a man, came to be among us in love. When they nailed Jesus to a cross, He refused to defy and amaze those who mocked Him by tapping into His power and miraculously coming down from the cross as they had challenged Him to do. Instead, His love for us made Jesus submissive, even unto death (Phil. 2:8).

Nietzsche was right: Love creates vulnerability and can get you crucified. Jesus is proof of that. Love requires enormous risk taking, and only those who are willing to risk vulnerability can experience it. Those who are unwilling to risk being hurt can never love.

When raising children, the same decision must be made. Are we going to use power to control them or are we going to lovingly woo them into being and doing what is right and what is good for them? I don't know about you, but I want children to obey their parents out of love, rather than out of fear. All too frequently, parents, who are bigger and stronger, depend on physical force to get their children to comply with their expectations, even though most of these parents know that this will only cause their children to grow into adults who all too readily resort to physical abuse when dealing with *their* spouses and children.

Using power in corporal punishment generally doesn't accomplish what we think it will accomplish. In the end, it is love, rather than the power of a slap across the face, that will win the heart of a child. In the words of Scripture, "Love never fails" (1 Cor. 13:8 NKJV).

LOVE AND POWER IN
THE WORLD OF POLITICS

There is an irony to history that few of us recognize, which is that the course of history is ultimately determined by love, rather than power. Down through the ages, there have been those who, like Jesus Barabbas, have sought to change the world through the use of power. Napoleon, who thought that God was on the side that had the most cannons, and Hitler, who made Nietzsche's philosophy of "the will to power" a political ideology in his attempt to forge a Reich that would last a thousand years, are just two of those who believed that power would sound the final note of history. But history does not yield to power so easily. And although those who have power often seem to prosper, love stands in the shadows, keeping watch and waiting for its time to come.

Consider the fact that those who have done the most to change the world have done so not with coercive power, but by living out the love teachings of Jesus as given in the Sermon on the Mount. Mahatma Gandhi was one of them. He was a man who resisted the oppression of colonialism, not with guns, but with love. When they asked him how he expected the English to leave India, he said, "As friends." He led a liberation movement, and a week after he gained freedom from his so-called enemies, he was welcomed by them in London as a hero.

More recently, we can find the Christ principle of love in Martin Luther King, Jr. When those who espoused his philosophy of nonviolence marched for their freedom, from Selma toward Montgomery, Alabama, they were stopped at the bridge on the edge of town. Confronting them were police and national guardsmen, armed with their instruments of power. When the word was given to King's followers to turn back, they answered, "We've come too far to turn back now." The demonstrators got down on their knees to pray, fully aware of how vulnerable this made them. Then the sheriff's deputies waded into them, swinging their billy clubs, turning loose their attack dogs, and knocking people down with powerful bursts of water from fire hoses.

As I watched it all on live television, I knew at that moment in history that the civil rights movement had won. If anyone had asked me, "How do you figure that they have won? All I see are followers of Martin Luther King getting battered and beaten and even killed," I would have answered, "Those who follow the way of Jesus have a strange habit of rising again, because there is no power on earth that can keep love down. When all that can be done to destroy them has been done, they will rise again." Martin Luther King declared to his enemies, "If you beat us, we will love you! If you jail us, we will love you, and if you kill us, we will die loving you!" As history has testified, love indeed triumphs over power.

The ways of Jesus Barabbas die hard in the Christian community, even though they are diametrically opposed to what Jesus Christ was all about. Recently there have been those who figure that the way to impact society with Christian values is through the exercise of political power. They buy into a downsized version of the Taliban when they try, through the power of the state, to impose on others directives for issues of personal morality that rightfully should be decided by individuals. Romans 13:1–5 makes it clear that government is supposed to restrain evildoers who would hurt others. But when it comes to personal moral issues, Christians make a serious mistake when they try to regulate, through the use of political power, what people can and cannot do. In personal matters we ought to use loving persuasion, rather than powerful coercion, to get people to live according to what we believe is right.

There are those who want to make America into a Christian

nation via political means, and this frightens me. While I would like all Americans to believe and act like I think Christians should, the last thing I want is for people to be forced to do so because the government is policing them. I want people to freely choose what they believe and do, as long as it doesn't threaten the property or physical well-being of others.

LOVE AND POWER
WHEN FACING OUR ENEMIES

Strange as it may sound, it has become dangerous to quote Jesus Barjoseph in many churches since September 11. As we find ourselves threatened by al-Qaeda and face the possibility of terrorist attacks, many in the pews don't want to hear that we are supposed to love our enemies, do good to those who would harm us, and return good for evil (Matt. 5:44). Our reactions as a people to the events of that painfully memorable day have tended to be along the lines of Jesus Barabbas. We want to kill off our enemies. Our answer to terrorist attacks is, for the most part, to wipe out those terrorists. That seems like the only practical solution to the followers of Jesus Barabbas. The words of Jesus Barjoseph seem like unrealistic ideals—hardly the stuff that belongs in the realm of real politics. Jesus Barjoseph said that those who live by the sword die by the sword (Matt. 26:52), but we are likely to go along with Jesus Barabbas, who said that *only* those who live by the sword survive.

Stop and think for a moment. Does any of us really believe that killing terrorists will end terrorism? Don't we have to ask ourselves if our war on terrorism really isn't creating more terrorists?

You don't get rid of malaria by killing the mosquitoes that carry the disease. You get rid of malaria only by getting rid of the swamps in which those disease-carrying mosquitoes breed. So it is that, if we are going to be rid of terrorists, we have to eliminate those conditions in which terrorists are bred. We have to try to do something about the poverty and the injustices that feed the hostilities of would-be terrorists toward those who live in affluent indifference to their plight. We must address the injustices that people endure as the result of U.S. government policies that are beneficial to our economic well-being but unfair to those who suffer in the Third World. The next time you buy clothing that was made in some sweatshop in the Philippines or Thailand, ought you not to be asking if the bargain you got was at the expense of some exploited child worker?

Our failure to do right by those who work to give us our taken-for-granted consumer goods is part of what causes terrorism. So many of the poor of the world hate us because they perceive, rightly or wrongly, that our good life is at their expense. We have to deal with that. When our way of life is seen as responsible for the poverty of people in poor countries, ought we not to remember that the Scriptures tell us that God especially cares for the poor (James 2:5)?

WILL LOVE REALLY WORK?

Recent studies on terrorism point out that suicide bombers have in common a mentality of hopelessness and deep resentment that arises from humiliation. When armed soldiers strip-search their grandfathers, force their fathers to lie facedown on the ground, and subject them to verbal abuse, the desperate anger that is generated can lead to violent reactions. It is our task to defend people's dignity and affirm their humanity.

There are those who will argue that love won't work when the adversaries are people who are hardened and without conscience. What such cynics do not recognize is that love can sometimes humanize adversaries and even bring them to repentance. But even when love does not win over those who have the power, love has a power of its own. Consider the case of Metropolitan Kyril, the leader of the Orthodox church in Bulgaria, and his heroic love for the Jewish people.

Even though Bulgaria was allied with Nazi Germany during World War II, not a single Bulgarian Jew ever died in a concentration camp. This was largely due to the stand that Bulgarian Christians took against the possible persecution of Jews by the SS troops. Of particular importance in their struggle against the Nazis was the heroism of Metropolitan Kyril.

At one time, the Nazis rounded up hundreds of Jews and had them imprisoned behind barbed-wire enclosures at the train station in Sophia. Soon a train would arrive, and the Jews would be squeezed into boxcars and shipped off to Auschwitz and almost certain death.

As the panic-stricken Jews, many sobbing hysterically, awaited their fate, a strange image appeared out of the drizzly, misty night. It was Metropolitan Kyril. He was a tall man to start with, but the miter that an Orthodox prelate wears on his head made him look like a giant. His flowing white beard hung down over his black robe, and it is said that his gait was such that the couple of hundred men who followed him had to hustle hard to keep up with him.

As he approached the entrance of the barbed-wire enclosure, the SS guards raised their machine guns and told him, "Father, you cannot go in there!" Metropolitan Kyril defiantly laughed at them, brushed aside the guns, and went into the midst of the Jewish prisoners. The apparently doomed Jews gathered around him, wondering what a leader of the Christian community would have to say to them at this desperate time. With arms upraised, Metropolitan Kyril recited one verse of Scripture from the book of Ruth. He helped to change the destiny of a nation as he shouted, "Whithersoever you go, I will go! Your people will be my people! Your God will be my God!"

With these words, the frightened Jews were suddenly turned into an emboldened mob. They cheered their Christian friend. The Christians on the outside of the barbed wire enclosures cheered with them, and they became one in the Spirit. Responding to the noise at the train station, the townspeople came out of their houses and joined the crowd.

The SS troops, surveying the scene, decided that discretion was the better part of valor. They boarded the train without their captives and left the town. What further evidence do we need to make the case that God's love can provide the motivation for history-changing action?

FOUR

LOVE CAN DO AMAZING THINGS

"Verily, verily, I say unto you, He that believeth on me, the works that I do shall he do also; and greater works than these shall he do; because I go unto my Father" (John 14:12).

When I was a boy, I found this promise made by Jesus very confusing. Sure, I believed in miracles. My mom had told me about miracles—some healings that had come about because of prayer—and I believed her. I had seen faith healers on television, and though some of their antics raised questions in my mind, I was nevertheless convinced that they were involved in something supernatural. But I knew of no one who could match the mighty works of Jesus Barjoseph. When I thought about Him raising the dead, making the blind to see and the lame to walk, changing water into wine, and all the other signs and wonders that the Bible says He did, I knew that even the best of the modern-day miracle workers couldn't match the awesome works of Jesus Christ. Yet there it was—the promise that what He did, we would be able to do. And if that were not enough, He went on to say, "And *greater* works than these shall he do" (v. 12; emphasis mine).

I remember asking my pastor, "How come none of us today can do what Jesus did, since He promised that we'd be able to?" My pastor answered that it was because we didn't have enough faith. He told me that all things were possible if we only believed. If we only had enough faith, he contended, we could remove mountains, just like Jesus Barjoseph said we could. That answer did not cut it with me. As far as I was concerned, there were no conditions on the Lord's promise. As I read that verse, Jesus Barjoseph declared that we *would* do greater works than He did—and it just wasn't happening. I thought my pastor's answer was a cop-out.

I handled that question like I did many of the things I found in the Bible that I didn't understand. I simply "bracketed" it, assuming it was one of those things I would never understand this side of glory.

Then one day, it hit me! It was one of those "Aha!" experiences in which something that previously made no sense suddenly becomes clear—and you wonder how you ever missed it in the first place. I realized that this verse was not referring to miracles at all. Instead, Jesus was referring to something much more important. He was not talking about the *power* demonstrated by His miracles, but rather the *love* inherent in each miracle—love for a man or woman in desperate need of help. Jesus Barjoseph was telling His disciples that the works they would do would be the works of *love*. Suddenly it became abundantly clear that He was trying to get His disciples to understand that soon He would leave them and ascend into heaven. Then He would return and be an indwelling spiritual presence who would dwell in each and every Christian, and through them He would do His works of love. It was works of love that He was talking about in this verse.

Consider this! The Son of God always was—even before the creation of the cosmos. Then, two thousand years ago, the eternal Christ took on a human body. He became the baby Jesus Barjoseph. He was born in Bethlehem's manger and grew up in Nazareth. Jesus Barjoseph became the body in which the eternal Christ dwelt and lived among us for more than thirty years. The Apostles' Creed tells us that He was crucified, dead, and buried, and that on the third day He rose from the grave and ascended to be at the right hand of the Father. But before He left us, this same eternal Christ, who was incarnated in Jesus Barjoseph, promised to come back and spiritually invade anyone who would willingly surrender to Him. Those who, in the depths of their being, would yield to the transforming effects of His Spirit could then become the "now" body of Christ. The same Spirit of Christ that was in Jesus Barjoseph could then dwell in the mortal bodies of any who would surrender to Him and become sons and daughters of God (John 1:12), just as Jesus Barjoseph was the "then" body of Christ two thousand years ago. The works of love that Jesus did back there and then, we can do today if the same Christ who was in Jesus Barjoseph dwells in us (John 14:12).

When the eternal Christ was historically incarnate in Jesus Barjoseph, He had some significant self-imposed human limitations. If He were looking lovingly into the eyes of Peter, He could not be looking into the eyes of John. If He were connecting with Mary in a face-to-face, loving relationship, He was not at the same time in such a face-to-face encounter with Martha. Jesus Barjoseph was able to have a personal encounter of love with only one person at a time.

But after His resurrection, Jesus Barjoseph ascended into

heaven as He said He would, and this same Christ came back and became a spiritual presence in all who would receive Him (John 15:1–7). The same Spirit that was in Jesus Barjoseph can be in each and every one of us (Rom. 8:1). Today tens of millions of people have invited Him into their lives. How many persons can tens of millions of Christians encounter face-to-face with Christ's love at any given moment? The answer is obvious: tens of millions! Are tens of millions greater than one? Of course! That is why Jesus Christ said, "The works that I do shall he do also; and greater works than these shall he do; because I go unto my Father." The millions who now make up the body of Christ are capable at any given moment of connecting in love, person to person, with millions of love-starved people all over the world. And you are invited to be part of this "now" body of Christ and to do the works of love that Christ did when He was here as Jesus Barjoseph of Nazareth.

THE HEALING WORKS OF LOVE

A number of years ago, I was a faculty member at the University of Pennsylvania. One evening, after leaving my lecture hall and heading for the parking lot to get my car, I met up with the Duck Lady. Just about everyone at Penn knew about the Duck Lady, a homeless woman who wandered around the campus. We called her the Duck Lady because she made an incessant quacking noise.

That particular evening, as I waited for a traffic light to change at the corner of 34th and Spruce Streets, I heard her coming. The quacking got louder and louder until there she was, alongside of me. I don't know why I did it, but I turned and looked into her eyes. I didn't look at her—I looked *into* her. I looked into her with all the spiritual energy that was in me. I felt myself reaching through her eyes into the depths of her being. In some mystical way I connected with her soul. Miracles like that do happen! There was a oneness between us. I *felt* it! We were one in the Spirit. I sensed myself loving her, and, to my surprise, I sensed that she was loving me back.

She stopped her quacking! I had never known her to stop quacking before, but she stopped! Then she looked around at the trees and sky, and she said slowly, with an air of wonder, "It's lovely! It's lovely! It's really lovely!"

The traffic light changed. Someone brushing by the woman bumped her. I noticed her head snap ever so slightly, and then she fell back into her previous schizophrenic condition. She started quacking again. I watched her as she wandered off, disappearing into a crowd of people—and I asked myself, *What might have happened if I had been able to love her just a little longer?* I wondered if we had remained transfixed for just a minute or two more whether her deliverance might have been more lasting.

I am a social scientist who believes in the good work that psychiatrists and psychotherapists can do for schizophrenics. But when they have done their best and failed, I do not say there is no hope. I believe there is still a balm in Gilead that can heal a troubled soul. In my brief encounter with the Duck Lady, I think that Jesus Barjoseph was saying, "The works that I did, you are doing."

Such a work of love may not be as dramatic as the miracles Jesus Barjoseph performed, but there is little doubt that it is just as significant. Consider the reality that none of His miracles had any permanence, save for His own resurrection. He raised Lazarus from the dead, but that had no lasting effect. What happened to Lazarus? He eventually died! One afternoon Jesus Christ fed five thousand people with just a few fish and a few loaves of bread. Guess what happened the next day? They were hungry!

All of the miracles of Jesus Barjoseph were brilliant displays of His power, but there was something far more important about them. Love was the reason for those miracles. I am not putting down miracles; they are signs of the kingdom of God that is to come. They are a foretaste of what life will be like one day—someday—when we are transformed into the new realm of being that Jesus Barjoseph has prepared for us. In that new world, there will be no sickness or death, and miracles point to the wholeness of life that all will enjoy in His kingdom. But we are not there yet! If you are blessed and miraculously cured of some life-threatening illness, I have some bad news—you are going to die anyway. But if you are yielded to Him and have become an instrument of His love, though you may die, you will live (John 11:25). That's a promise!

THE SAVING WORKS OF LOVE

Love was always more crucial than power when it came to the saving work of Jesus. Even now, Jesus Barjoseph does not use His power to force anyone to become part of His kingdom, but instead tries to woo us with His love. When considering how He would save the world, He said, "I, if I be lifted up from the earth [i.e., crucified], will draw all men [and women] unto me" (John 12:32). Jesus Barjoseph wants to draw us to Him with love rather than play power games with us.

The Jesus whom we worship has always been about love. As God incarnate, certainly He had power at His disposal, but that was not to be His means for saving the world. Satan tried to get the Son of God to accomplish His salvation through power rather than through love during the temptation in the wilderness (Luke 4:1–13), but Jesus Barjoseph would not take that route, lest He be reduced to the likes of Jesus Barabbas. He chose to win people to Himself with sacrificial love rather than with displays of power.

Consider how often Jesus Barjoseph sought to downplay the power He used when love constrained Him to perform miracles. As a case in point, consider His first miracle: turning water into wine at the wedding feast at Cana (John 2:1–10). Jesus Barjoseph was there with His disciples. His mother was there, too. And, in the midst of the festivities, Mary noticed something that was extremely troubling. Those in charge of the wedding feast were running out of wine! In those days, to have prepared inadequately for your daughter's wedding was to be publicly disgraced. The father of the bride may have been pacing the floor, wringing his hands and saying, "I thought I had enough wine. I used up all of my assets and even mortgaged the house to buy the wine that was needed." Perhaps the bride knew what was happening and had been reduced to tears. This was supposed to be the best day of her life, and it was being ruined. The groom, no doubt, was beside himself trying to figure out what to do.

Then Mary went over to her son and asked for a miracle—and He didn't want to do it. He wanted to avoid the fame that goes with the power of being a miracle worker. But at His mother's urging, Jesus Barjoseph responded by calling for the servants to fill some large jars with water—and then He turned the water into wine.

Please note that Jesus Barjoseph told the servants who had witnessed the miracle to keep quiet about what they had seen. He did not want people to know about His power. What He did, He did out of love. His love for a distraught father, a heartbroken bride, and a confused groom prompted Jesus Barjoseph to use His power, but the miracle was really about His love for those people.

Consider the miracle of Nain, when Jesus Barjoseph raised a young man from the dead (Luke 7:11–15). As He approached the town, He and His disciples came upon a funeral. The dead man was the only son of a woman who had already been widowed. In the ancient world in which she lived, there was no way for her to survive without a husband or son to support her financially. Jesus Barjoseph took the dead son's hand and miraculously gave life back to him. He did it, not to show off His power, but because of His great love for the woman.

There were other times when Jesus Barjoseph asked those who had been blessed by His miracles not to broadcast what He had done. For example, when He healed a certain blind man, Jesus Barjoseph told him to keep quiet about it. I believe that, in such instances, Jesus Barjoseph was trying to keep the demonstrations of His power from overshadowing the salvation story of His love.

THE MORE EXCELLENT WAY

This understanding of Jesus Barjoseph that sees in Him the primacy of love over power is not just mine. The apostle Paul certainly knew this to be true. Paul had witnessed signs and wonders and spoke glowingly of those who could perform miracles, but he recognized that the expression of love was far more important. Paul knew the validity of miracles, but when he wrote the famous thirteenth chapter of 1 Corinthians, he put love in front of any of the signs and wonders that demonstrates God's power. He acknowledged that miracles happen by the grace of God, but then he went on to say that there was "a more excellent way" to show what Jesus Barjoseph and those who would follow Him were really all about; and that was love in action (1 Cor. 12:31).

Today there are those who preach what has been called power evangelism, contending that performing signs and wonders should very much be a part of proclaiming the gospel. Far be it from me to criticize any attempt to create an openness to the gospel by showing miraculous healings to nonbelievers. I know of people who have come to Christ because they were first awed by such signs and wonders. It is just that I believe the world is *more* hungry to see the love of God expressed in us and through us than it is to be dazzled by miracles that show off God's power.

I have found that even when skeptics have miracles thrown in their faces, they often have a great capacity to discount them by attributing the miraculous to some natural cause. When I was in graduate school, my major professor, Paul Van Buren, was not willing to accept that anything that defied the laws of empirical science could ever happen. One day he said to me, "Tony, if you're such a believer in miracles, why don't you go out on the Commons and build an altar of wood like Elijah did in the Hebrew Bible? Then call out all the agnostics and atheists of the university to watch you do what Elijah is supposed to have done. Douse the wood with water and prove to the skeptics that there is a God by praying down fire from heaven to consume the altar."

I didn't have a good answer for him, but I did have a question. "Dr. Van Buren," I asked, "suppose I did exactly as you suggested, and fire did come down from heaven and consume the water-soaked altar. Would you then believe in God?" He thought for a while and then answered wryly, "I'd probably say that there must be another explanation."

Miracles don't always convince nonbelievers to change their ways of thinking and acting. Jesus Barjoseph said as much when He told the story of the rich man and Lazarus (Luke 16:19–31). When the rich man realized that his lost condition in hell had no remedy, he begged Abraham to send Lazarus back from the dead, convinced that such an awesome miracle would compel his sinful brothers to change their ways. Jesus answered that if they would not be convinced by Scripture, they would not be convinced even if someone should rise from the dead.

When Jesus Barjoseph was being crucified, those who

mocked Him called upon Him to provide a miracle and come down from the cross. They cried out that if Jesus Barjoseph could pull that off, then they would believe in Him. But He refused. Even then, He would not play the power game. Instead, He sought to win the lost through the drawing effects of His sacrificial love. In the end, Jesus Barjoseph chose sacrificial love rather than power as His means for saving the world.

THE GREATER WORKS OF LOVE

For all of us who do not seem to be able to provide miracles for an unbelieving world, there is the good news of an even better way to bring people into God's kingdom, and that is to love them there. Miracles are good, but love is better! Jesus Barjoseph calls us to do works of love in our own time, even as He did works of love in His time. He promises that the works of love that He did, we will be able to do, because He has gone to the right hand of His Father and will come back to those who will receive Him, be an indwelling presence in them, and, through them, continue to live out love in the world. And, because we are many, together we will do even greater works than Jesus Barjoseph did two thousand years ago.

One evening I sat in the terminal of a small airport in Farmington, New Mexico, waiting for a commuter plane to carry me to Denver for a connecting flight home. I noticed an old woman sitting alone. From her expression, she appeared to be mad at the world. Having nothing else to do, I decided to sit next to her, try to strike up a conversation, and, if possible, get her to smile. It worked! Not only did I get her to smile, but I got her to laugh! It was like an emotional dike had been broken, because once she started laughing, there was no stopping her. The few other men in the small waiting room gathered around the two of us, and soon we were all having a hilarious time. When the awaited commuter plane finally landed, the friend for whom the old lady had been waiting disembarked. The two of them hugged each other, bade us good-bye, left the terminal, and drove away.

As I waited for the announcement to board my plane, I happened to look out the glass doors of the terminal, and I saw the old lady's car coming back up the driveway. She got out of the car and, with measured steps, walked up to me. "Mister," she said, "it was two years ago today that my husband of fifty-four years died. You couldn't have known that. But as I was on my way home, I realized that today is the first day since then that I've been able to laugh, and I just had to come back and thank you."

And Jesus said, "The works that I do shall he do also; and greater works than these shall he do; because I go unto my Father."

FIVE

LOVE'S SUPREMACY
OVER POWER

All of this talk about giving love priority over power and contending that signs and wonders are real, as they might be, is all well and good until we are desperate for a miracle to happen. When a mother is dying of cancer and will leave small children behind, we crave a Jesus who will use His power to cure her. If a man finds himself facing the ruin of his reputation and the destruction of his family, he prays for a miracle to save him. The parents who feel helpless when it comes to turning a son or daughter away from a path that will lead to sin and death want a God who will miraculously intercede for them and turn that child around. But, sadly, in most such cases, miracles do not happen. Oh, there are those who tell us that the God who was revealed in Jesus Barjoseph never fails to deliver miracles if we just pray the right way and end our prayers with the right words. But those who find themselves in desperate straits and see a miracle as their only hope are, more often than we like to admit, disappointed.

In the midst of our disappointments with God, we try to come up with rationalizations that will make God look good, even in the face of tragedies that we believe God could have prevented. Sometimes we try to put a good spin on our disappointments by saying that what we wanted just wasn't God's will. But deep down inside we are likely to wonder why a God of love whom we believe has the power to make things right didn't act to do so.

More painful may be the latent fear that the reason the desperately needed miracle did not happen was because the people who prayed did not have enough faith. Now I am not saying that there aren't some verses of Scripture to back up such a painful belief; it's just that, as a case in point, I have trouble believing in a God sitting in the heavens and saying that the agonizing suffering of an innocent child could be eradicated if the parents just had greater intensity of faith in their prayers. I have witnessed too many good people on guilt trips because they think their lack of faith caused the suffering and death of someone whom they desperately loved.

Maybe it's time for us to understand that the Jesus Barjoseph to whom we pray doesn't always use His power to work the miracles we crave because He has chosen to set aside that power and make love His means for salvation. Maybe we have to realize that we can't have it both ways and that in choosing the way of sacrificial love, He has had to set aside the way of power. As has already been pointed out, it is close to impossible to express love and utilize power at the same time. To love, Jesus Barjoseph had to put limits on His power. And for us to have the freedom to love Him and to love one another, He had to give up control over our decision making and let us embrace Him and one another as we will. Love can never be coerced. God, in Jesus Barjoseph, chose out of love to set aside power. We have a God right now whose power is not all that we might want it to be but whose love has no limits.

Suffering and death are the prices we pay for living in a world in which Jesus Barjoseph has set aside His power to come to us in love and give us the freedom either to love Him and others or to play our futile power games with each other. I say that our power games are futile because even if we reject the Jesus Barjoseph who is at work in the world exercising His love, He *is* coming back again. And the next time He breaks into history, He will take up His power and destroy that which refuses to surrender to His love.

POWER TEMPERED BY LOVE

There will be some who ask, "If God is somehow limited because of a commitment to work in the world through love, then what can God offer when a miracle is needed?"

Let me try to be very clear as I answer that question, because a lot is at stake. To start with, it is way beyond me even to try to explain what God can and cannot do, or what God will and will not do. God, as Søren Kierkegaard rightly says, is "totally other." That means that God's ways of thinking and acting are way beyond anything that we can comprehend. However, within the realm of human understanding, I have to say we can't have it both ways. If we want a God who is all-powerful and controls everything, we may have to give up a God who works through love.

Love and power, as I pointed out earlier, stand opposed. The expressing of love requires the setting aside of power, which is just what God did. In Christ, God became one of us, and in the weakness that goes with becoming the suffering servant and the savior prophesied by Isaiah, God's power was set aside. That choice, made by God, is what the apostle Paul described in Philippians 2:5–10 when he wrote that in Christ, God gave up the prerogative of power and became as powerless as a slave. Jesus Barjoseph is the God who is at work among us, saving us through sacrificial love, and His way of saving the world is through a cross.

There may be times when we wish that Jesus Barjoseph would be more like Jesus Barabbas and use His power, but such a God would have to deny us freedom. If God used power to control everything that goes on in our lives, we might be freed from the evils that plague us, but we would then be reduced to puppets. Puppets cannot love, because to love requires free will. And Jesus Barjoseph wants our love, even though the cost for us, as well as for Himself, is incredibly high. In our everyday lives we can find a host of examples wherein love requires that help be withheld from someone who suffers.

Consider the case of a particular child who, because of the misuse of the drug thalidomide, was born without any arms. As the boy grew, his mother taught him to do a variety of rather complex things with his feet, including writing, eating, and even playing the guitar. The most difficult everyday task for him was learning how to dress himself. Trying as hard as she could, his mother just was not able to get him to do this. Every morning he begged for her help, and every morning she came to the rescue. Then one day, she made an extremely difficult decision. She put his clothes on his bed and told him that she would not let him out of his room until he dressed himself.

He begged for help as he struggled with his clothes. He screamed at her and accused her of not really loving him. He stomped about the room, kicking whatever he could and shouting obscenities. And all day long his mother sat outside the locked door, crying. Less love would have had her intervene, but great love left her with no alternative but to force her son into the struggle that goes with independence. In telling this story he now says that only in retrospect did he realize how much love it took for his mother to make him into a free man.

God, because of love, often refuses to step in and use power to deal with the agonies of our existence. During most times of suffering, all that we get from God are empathetic tears—and they are tears that cannot be heard. That silence can seem unbearable, but the tears of God are real.

One of America's most prominent preachers, William Sloan Coffin, lost his son because of a mountain-climbing accident. When, during the funeral, the clergyman conducting the service said, "This is all part of God's great plan," Coffin stood and called out, "No, it's not! When my son died, God was the first one who cried."

The shortest verse in the Bible tells us that Jesus Barjoseph wept (John 11:35). I believe that He continues to weep as He empathizes with all of those who suffer. Understanding that Jesus sheds tears for us is a source of comfort and strength, and it may be all we have to carry us through our darkest days. When the storms of life beat upon us, as the Scriptures say they will, Jesus Barjoseph does not appear at our bidding to drive our troubles away. But, if we are grounded in His promises, we will have a solid spiritual foundation undergirding us that will enable us to endure those storms. During those times, when Jesus is all we have, we will know that He is all we need.

JESUS' POWER REVEALED IN HIS SECOND COMING

The Scriptures and the Apostles' Creed declare that the same Jesus Barjoseph who ascended into heaven forty days after His resurrection from the dead is coming back again. And the Bible tells us that when He comes the next time, He will be coming in power. With power He will destroy all who refuse to be changed through love. The Lamb of God, Jesus Barjoseph, will again take up the power He once set aside and come back as the Lion of Judah. On that awesome day, those who stand against Him will face dire consequences.

Upon His second coming, the world that is will be transformed into the world that it was meant to become when it was first created. The political and economic institutions that today seem so rife with evil will be brought under His lordship, and He shall reign over them forever and ever (Rev. 15).

There is nothing inherently wrong with power. While it has a corrupting influence on fallible people, our Jesus Barjoseph, who is without sin, can use it without it destroying Himself. The point I have been making is that it is difficult, and usually impossible, to express love and power at the same time. But power can be used for good. For everything there is a season (Eccles. 3:1). Presently, with His love, Jesus Barjoseph redeems and renews the world. But the day is coming when, with His power, He will establish order over a world that demonic forces have made chaotic, and He will put down evil and death forever (1 Cor. 15:24–28). Even now there are signs of His coming reign. His miracles are a foretaste of that kingdom wherein sickness and death will be no more, and all tears shall be wiped away.

Miracles are not normative, but every now and then Jesus Barjoseph gives us a foretaste of His coming kingdom and heals someone supernaturally. Such miracles are only signs of what is to come. They offer no permanent solution to the agonies of sickness and death that are woven into the fabric of the here and now. If you should be so fortunate as to experience God's power through some miracle that destroys an ugly consequence of living in this fallen world, you still have to face the reality that you will die anyway. Sooner or later, the painful consequences of being part of this present age will take hold of you. But don't let that defeat you. The day is coming when the loving Jesus Barjoseph will again take up His power and subdue the sickness and death that threaten your joy. Then, miracles will not be needed to give you a glimpse of His coming kingdom. Then, the skies will roll back as a scroll, the Lord shall descend, and all evil and sadness will be abolished. And then, Jesus Barjoseph will be King!

SIX

HOW TO EXPERIENCE
THE MIRACLE OF LOVE

Anyone who is willing to be transformed by Jesus Barjoseph's indwelling presence can become a new creation who can transcend the will to power and relate to others in love. Each of us can become a channel through whom Christ's love can be focused on others.

How do we experience the miracle of love? *It all begins with prayer!* I am not talking about the kind of prayer that is little more than the reading off of a list of demands to the Almighty. Instead, I am referring to the kind of prayer that Jesus Barjoseph was talking about as He directed His followers to go into a closet, shut the door, and experience the overpowering presence of God in a dark and quiet secret place.

Jesus Barjoseph scorned the prayers of the Pharisees in

His day because they sought the admiration of others with high-sounding pieties and vain repetitions. He opted for more contemplative prayers that lead to a sense of mystical oneness with God. He told His disciples to go into the closet to pray because, in order to connect with God, it is best to escape the distractions around us. Contrary to popular opinion, going outdoors to pray amidst the beauties of nature is not always a good idea. To sit in a lovely place and absorb the beauty of God's creation is certainly a deeply spiritual experience, but if you want to know the deeper kind of prayer that Jesus Barjoseph was talking about, you probably need to escape the distractions of natural beauty. It is in solitude and darkness that you will learn how to pray those special prayers that the apostle Paul called "groanings which cannot be uttered" (Rom. 8:26).

PRAYING IN THE SPIRIT

Most of us are familiar with prayers wherein we petition God to meet our needs or, in our more selfish times, ask for what we want. All of us can tell stories about miracles that have resulted from such prayers, as the Scriptures say they will (James 5:16). Through prayer the sick have been healed, the souls of loved ones have been touched, and troubling circumstances have been changed for the better. As the poet Alfred Lord Tennyson said so well, "More things are wrought by prayer, than this world dreams of."

Yet prayer must never be self-centered, nor should we treat God as some kind of transcendental Santa Claus who will deliver what we want if we are good. That is why Jesus Barjoseph said to pray in His name (John 14:13–14). To pray in the name of Jesus Barjoseph is to take on the consciousness of Jesus Barjoseph. It is to have in you that mind which was also in Christ Jesus (Phil. 2:5). Praying in the name of Jesus Barjoseph is an essential ministry that each of us is called upon to render for the sake of others as well as to supply ourselves with what God wants us to have.

But there is another kind of prayer wherein the Holy Spirit prays *through* us. It is a special kind of praying that occurs when we surrender in quietude and the Holy Spirit gains control of what goes on in our hearts and minds (Rom. 8:26). This is called "praying in the Spirit," and when we do it, something happens to us. We become infused with God, and hence we become infused with love—because God is love.

For me, praying in the Spirit is best done early in the morning. In the darkness of the early hours, I lie still and wait patiently for Jesus Barjoseph to come and love me. I repeat His name over and over again. I do that in order to drive back any distractions and because there is something mystical that happens when I repetitiously intone His name in the stillness of the morning.

Sometimes the inner stillness comes over me in a minute or two, but usually it takes much longer. Sometimes it doesn't come at all. Yet when the Spirit breaks in, I feel an expansion of my soul. You may have to wait patiently on the Lord several times before you experience this refreshing awareness of God. But it *does* happen! The Spirit will blow upon you! As the Bible says, the Holy Spirit is like the wind, and you cannot tell from whence it comes or where it goes (John 3:8). The Holy Spirit cannot be controlled, but you can prepare for the coming of the Spirit by making yourself inwardly still and patiently waiting. We have God's promise that if we truly seek Him, we will find Him (Luke 11:9).

CONNECTING IN THE ETERNAL NOW

Of all that happens to me in prayer, first and foremost the Spirit connects me with the Jesus Barjoseph who hangs on the cross. In this special stillness, the two thousand years separating me from the cross on Calvary's hill no longer exist. The two events—me in the existential now, and Jesus Barjoseph hanging on the cross back there and then—are compressed into what philosophers and theologians sometimes call "the eternal now."

In the natural world, time is a linear progression, a sequence of events occurring in a historically defined order that the ancient Greeks called *chronos.* But when, in sacred stillness, I transcend the natural order of things, I enter into God's time, called *kairos,* wherein all things become simultaneous, since God transcends time and space.

Those who are into modern physics know that time is not the fixed thing we usually think it is. Time, according to Einstein, is relative to motion. Einstein said that as we speed up, time becomes increasingly compressed until, at the speed of light, it is compressed into simultaneity. The motion picture *Contact* conveyed this concept. In that film, Jody Foster's character is reluctant to take a space journey to another galaxy because she would be traveling so fast that earthly time would be compressed for her, and when she returned her lover would be much older than she would be—and might even be dead. At the speed of light, according to Einstein, all of time would be compressed into one "eternal now."

Because Jesus Barjoseph was not only a man but also God incarnate, I believe that He was able to experience time like that. He was, and is, able to experience everything that ever happened or will happen, at one time. And that is why I believe that Jesus Barjoseph on the cross is able to be simultaneous with me as I pray in the "now." He is the great I AM. Jesus Barjoseph never "was" nor ever "will be." There is no past or present with Him. He is the Alpha and the Omega—the beginning and the end of time (Rev. 1:8). In His divinity, Jesus Barjoseph is always in the now. With Him a thousand years are as a day, and a day as a thousand years (2 Pet. 3:8). That is why He could say, "Before Abraham *was,* I *am*" (John 8:58; emphasis mine).

In the stillness of the eternal now, I become aware of my connectedness with Him. In that spiritual connectedness, I sense Jesus Barjoseph taking all of my sin away from me. In this stillness, I experience an inner cleansing of my soul as I confess those things in me that I know have grieved the Holy Spirit. Then the Holy Spirit, long suppressed by my sin, explodes within my soul; and the fruit of the Spirit, including joy, peace, and most of all love, flood my soul (Gal. 5:22). This love that fills my soul is an expansive dynamic energy that at times constrains me to give it away to others.

The Love of the Spirit

This love that comes from praying in the Spirit is more than an emotion; it is a compelling presence that must be expressed in actions. That is why, all through Scripture, love is something that you and I are commanded to *do*: "You shall love the Lord your God!" "You shall love your neighbor!" "Love your enemies!"

Love is a sanctified way of relating to others. Hassidic philosopher Martin Buber helps to explain this spiritualized love. He contends that, in our everyday encounters, people too often treat each other as objects, things to be manipulated to serve egoistic interests. In other words, people "use" each other. However, the love that flows from God does not treat other persons as things to be used. It offers oneness with other persons that abolishes loneliness and overcomes alienation.

In an encounter created by love, you no longer look merely *at* the other person. Instead, you look *into* the other person. With the loving energy imparted to you by the Spirit, you can look *into* another person's eyes and even reach down into his or her soul. You can feel your way into the other person's being and come to know the other, even as you know yourself. The other person not only feels your love, but also feels the love of God flowing through you into him or her. The two of you find yourselves bound together with God in the midst of you (Matt. 18:20).

Loving another person with this kind of spiritual connectedness can have therapeutic consequences. Do you know a child who needs deliverance from a lifestyle of destructive rebellion? Loving that child in the Spirit may offer the best hope for his or her deliverance.

Do you have a husband or a wife who has lost the capacity for joy and is living in quiet desperation? Entering into the depths of that partner's heart, mind, and soul through Spirit-generated love may bring renewal to that person and a new life to your marriage.

Do you have a friend who has been betrayed and left with a deep-rooted bitterness? The love of God given through you to that friend might be just what your friend needs to be healed and restored to a sense of inner peace.

If you begin to share this kind of love with whomever God places in your path, you will find that such encounters can quench the thirst for acceptance, satisfy the hunger for affection, and impart a sense of being understood at the deepest levels of personhood.

ARE YOU READY TO DO LOVE?

The promise that Jesus Barjoseph made to His disciples can be valid for you, and you can embrace love as a way of life. You, too, can do what He called "greater works" and live out love at home, in the workplace, and in the midst of our world of trouble and strife. But you must be willing to abandon power in your relationships with others. Coercion is not the way of love. To be a conduit of the love of Jesus Christ, you must be willing to say yes to these questions.

First, are you willing to invite Jesus to change you from what you are into what He wants you to be? Do you want Him to remove the sin from your soul as you ask Him to cleanse you?

Your body is a temple waiting for the indwelling presence of the Holy Spirit. But the Spirit is holy and will not dwell in a dirty temple. Are you really ready to let go of those pleasurable sins that frustrate God's desire to fill you with the Holy Spirit? Or are you like Saint Augustine, who once prayed, "Oh God, deliver me from lust—but not yet!" Only to the extent that you are ready to be freed from sin will you be free to welcome that Spirit that generates love and sets love into action. Only then can you become a person through whom Jesus can do His "greater works."

Second, are you willing to commit the time required for daily infillings of the Holy Spirit? Being filled with the Spirit is a daily thing, and it takes time. Are you ready to take time each day to withdraw from the world around you and allow quietude to envelop you? Only then will the soft, still voice of God's Spirit that bears witness with your spirit convince you that you are loved by God.

The Scriptures say that you can love only if you first let God love you (1 John 4:19). Only those who feel God loving them are free to risk the vulnerability that loving others requires. It is not enough to accept the truth that God loves you. You must *experience* it daily—for yourself. This requires setting aside time for intimacy with God. This is not time designated for Bible study, as important as that is. Nor is it time for asking God to meet your needs, as urgent as those needs may be. What I am asking here is, Are you ready to make time daily to submit to that stillness in which you can sense the all-encompassing love of God? Are you willing to wait patiently on the Lord? If you do, the Lord will enable you to love. Then when unloving people wear you down with their unresponsiveness to your gestures of love, you will have the grace to keep on walking with them, and you will not faint (Isa. 40:31).

Have you ever come in from a chilly, rainy night, soaked and shivering, and sat in front of a blazing fireplace? If you have, you will remember the comforting, penetrating warmth of the fire. So it can be with your quiet times of prayer. You can feel God's comforting presence, penetrating your soul and giving you a sense of spiritual warmth. You can feel, as Romans 8:16 says, God's Spirit bearing witness with your spirit that you are truly a child of God. This awareness of God will not always happen during your times of prayerful stillness, but that does not mean God is not there. There will be times that the saints have called times of dryness. But God is faithful, and His promise never to leave you or forsake you holds firm (Heb. 13:5). Keep at it, day after day. And remember that the Scriptures call upon us to wait patiently for the Lord (Ps. 40:1).

Third, are you willing to pay the price? There is no cheap grace for those who want to live out love in the world. Striving to become like Jesus Barjoseph will cost you all that you are and all that you have. It may mean leaving the comfort zone in which you have lived and venturing in "regions beyond," where your sacrificial service is needed. It may mean the loss of the financial security that you once trusted would give you inner peace. It may mean being scorned, even by some in your own household who think that living out love with Christlike abandon is carrying things too far (Matt. 10:35–36). But after all is said and done, you will hear applause from nail-pierced hands.

When Jesus Barjoseph asked His disciples if they were ready to be crucified with Him, those sturdy dreamers answered, "To the death we follow thee!" You may be wondering if you will be able to answer Him as fully as they did. If you are like me, probably not! But you can join me in trying. You can pray this prayer with me, and together we can start the transforming process whereby we can come to love, even as He loved.

Lord, make me willing to will Your will,
Make me ready to answer Your call.
I am not there yet.
Maybe I'll never get there this side of heaven,
But there is a hunger within me,
And I want You to increase that hunger,
So that all I want is to love You with all my heart,
With all my strength, and with all my mind.
I want to yield to You until my soul is wholly Yours.
I want You to pour Yourself into me so that I will be able
To love my neighbor and to do for my neighbor
Some of those greater works You promised I would do
When You left this world and ascended to Your Father.
I want to live so that when this life is over,
I will hear You say, "Well done, good and faithful servant."
Amen.

*The Contemporary Classics Series pairs classic works with a
CD of the original message that inspired the book*

It's Friday but Sunday's Comin'
by Tony Campolo

This classic book brings you face to face
with Dr. Campolo to hear an unashamed
proclamation that the Gospel of Christ,
when taken seriously, is able to meet
every human need.

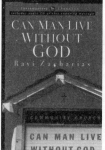

Can Man Live Without God?
Ravi Zacharias

In this brilliant and compelling defense
of the Christian faith, Ravi Zacharias
shows how affirming the reality of God
matters urgently in our everyday lives.

Improving Your Serve
Charles Swindoll

In this classic volume, Charles Swindoll
uniquely shows the important aspects of
authentic servanthood.

W PUBLISHING GROUP™
www.wpublishinggroup.com